Leicestershire
Myth and Legend
'In Verse'

Phil Simpkin

'If history were taught in the form of stories, it would never be forgotten.'

Rudyard Kipling.

Dedication

This book of storytelling verse is dedicated to my wonderful Grand-children

Ruby; Maxwell; Owen; Kallum and Dean

I hope in the future they may cherish folklore and have a greater understanding of some of the old tales of the County in which they have been born and raised.

Introduction

These few poems were written by me, initially to be told or sung, in verse, as part of local 'Folk night' entertainment.

Procrastination being the thief of time, I have not got round to telling either way, and have them on my pile of 'things to do'.

Consequently, I have decided to share them in this little written collection.

I hope they may serve for entertainment, or may even offer some educational purpose, but they are meant to be fun.

Come gather, come gather, my friends gather round

Because tales of old Leicestershire Folk have I found

Please let me indulge you and tell just a few

So fill up you glasses with glorious brew

Some folk may be famous and well known to you

Some may be vague or divulge something new

Some tell of sad lives and are tragically true

Whilst others disclosed, seem bad through and through

So gather, come gather, my friends gather round

And I'll share with you all of these folk that I've found

So sup on your spirits, your wine or your ale

And let's settle down to some Leicestershire tales

There's Black Anis of course - I 'ope she ain't here

To spoil our few tales or curdle the beer

Jane Grey and John Merrick and one or two more

And Highwayman Davenport, friend of the poor

So gather, come gather, my friends gather round

And fill up your glasses and settle right down

Put a log on the fire and the wood in the hole

Soon we'll start with the witch and end up at the Pole!

Black Annis

Black Annis is the most prominent of Leicester's Myths and Legends when it comes to Witchcraft and Wizardry.

She is described as a blue faced hag, with iron claws, from which she dug out her Bower, or cave, in the Dane Hills area of Leicester, which is now covered by property on the top end of Glenfield Road.

She is part of the 'bogeyman' culture of the British Isles, but though seen as originating from Leicestershire, historians suggest she is more widely known of Celtic origins, and there are links to such a bogeyman, known as Black Annis, or Black Agnes, going back centuries, throughout England, Scotland and Ireland. She may also have Greek or Germanic connections.

At the Leicestershire level, there is a stronger suggestion that the legend originated from a religious 'Anchoress' by the name of Agnes Scott, who originally cared for a Leper colony, at the site at which a local Catholic Convent currently stands, close to where the Bower was located.

An Anchoress was a religious hermit. Agnes, lived in

isolation in the Bower, and the legend of stealing children spun out of folk lore as a means to keep the children away from this strange, reclusive woman.

Agnes sounds a devoted and caring woman, as opposed to the child stealing, flagellator of myth and legend, but a good story feeds on more than just good, and 'bad' makes more interesting reading.

So, Black Annis is portrayed as about as bad as it gets.

My late Grandfather was born at a place called Three Queens Lodge, on the Sewstern Drift, at Wyville, between Melton Mowbray and Grantham.

The Three Queens were allegedly ancient tribal queens, turned into trees by Annis, and they stood at the site until early in the Twentieth Century, when they and the Lodge were felled.

Old Annis knew her way around Leicestershire, for sure.

Here's my little tale in verse...

Black Annis, Black Annis, crawl back to your cave

For the children of Leicester want you in a grave

You suckle their blood and you steal their skins

For now seven hundred years, when this story begins

Black Annis' cave was a Bower in Dane Hills

Dug with her own nails, black and yellow and old

And outside stood a tree, from which she'd descend

And grab passing children or so it is told

Her skirt sewn from skin was foul, ragged and grim

Her bodice was bloodied and hairy her chin

She preyed on young sheep if a child wasn't found

As over the hedges and fields she did bound

Her Bower in Dane Hills, to many was Hell

Desolate, dirty and devilish smell

She had a great lover his name it was Bel

He has his own story, as I'll later tell

The two of them wandered the length of the land

And preyed upon everything living, to hand

In Ireland they're hated, in Scotland afeared

But their legend, is Leicestershire based it appears

Keep an eye on your daughters; keep an eye on your sons

And lock all your cat flaps, and windows and doors

Cos if Annis is prowling she's fearless and bold

If you leave a small gap it's the end, so we're told

Black Annis, Black Annis, crawl back to your cave

For the children of Leicester want you in a grave

You suckle their blood and you steal their skins

For seven hundred years you've committed your sins

ST 3/2013

Bel the Giant

Legends are divided on the story of Bel.

Many are based on the tales of a race of Giants that once inhabited the British Isles.

Others are more sinister, and Bel is seen as a derivation of Ba'al, or Beelzebub, the Devil himself, Old Nick!

The legend for the Giant version married Bel with other legends, such as Black Annis, who we have looked at, and who allegedly was his spouse.

He is also intrinsically linked to his magnificent horse, Sorrel and many of the place names that span the North and East of the City and County are attributed with names gained from this single legendary Giant.

Here is my short tale...

We've spoken of Bel once already in verse

As the lover of Annis, he is known

But his real name is Ba'al – the devil himself

Old Leicestershire once was his home

Bel had a companion – Sorrel - his horse

A huge heavy beast black as night

It dwelt to the north in fields no-one dare cross

Now Mountsorrel – where Bel mounted of course!

So legend will tell, he rode Sorrel like hell

Through Rothley and down by the river

Which he crossed with one leap and a roar from the horse

So Wanlip it's known as, of course

The beast gathered speed as it raced for Ba'al

A second mighty leap the beast tried

The beast's gall bladder burst, and his heart broke in two,

Hence the name of Birstall was contrived

The devils beast was still with breath

It rose to its feet and sighed

For a mile they rode on, til the horse fell again

Onto Bel it did roll – there both died!

To the residents there, the devil now gone

They wanted them out of the way

So they dug a large hole, which they buried them in

And Belgrave it is called still today!

Mountsorrel

Wanlip

Birstall

Belgrave

King Leir

According to the ancient scribe, Geoffrey of Monmouth, Leir was an ancient king of the Britons, who Shakespeare later wrote of in his eponymous play.

What is not widely known is that Leir was real and that his name was the source of the name of the city today, Leicester.

Originally known as Kaerleir or Caer Leir (Ancient Welsh) the seat of this king was located somewhere between the modern villages of Leire and Croft, alongside what was then a significant lake, along the banks of the River Soar.

The family was never happy. Leir had the three daughters spoken of by Shakespeare, and in the end, he was deposed and went off to Gaul, where he lived to his old age, before the Gauls restored him back to his rightful throne, here in Leicestershire.

Upon his death, his body is alleged to be buried in a tomb, under the River Soar, somewhere near to the current City Centre.

Perhaps unearthing his tomb might merit another project for archaeologists now that they have found 'the other King'?

Here is Leir's tale in verse.

Long before William Shakespeare

A play in Lear's name he did write

The real Leir came from Old Leicester

From his own name Leicester did derive

Leir - the son of King Blaudad

Who In Elijah - the prophet's — time reigned

Sixty years he was king, from the banks of the Soar

And his town he did name Kaerleir

Not a son did Leir breed for succession

But three daughters would vie for his throne

Cordelia, Goneril and Regan

Are the names by which known

There was never such unhappy family

All wanted their share of the Throne

Through marriage, betrayal, and division

King Leir was left on his own

Insanity came, and he strayed far away

To Gaul, where he lived through both old age and pain

But the Gaul's loved King Leir and thus brought him home,

Leir restored to his throne, once again

When death finally came, near to town he was laid

Janus's chamber his last place of rest

And once a year after, a feast in his name

Was upheld to remember the best

So when you now hear of the Bard's tale

Think more of the roots of such names

Think of Leire and the source of old Leicester

And now you will know whence they came

Lady Jane Grey

Born 1536, Died 12/2/1554.

Queen of England 10/7/1553 to 19/7/1553.

'The nine day Queen'.

Jane Grey was the eldest daughter of Henry Grey, 1st Duke of Suffolk.

She spent much of her early life at Bradgate Park in Leicestershire, where the ruins of the family home can still be seen today.

Contrary to popular belief, she was not born there, but in London.

She was the Great-Grand-daughter of Henry VII, and 1st Cousin to Edward VI.

She married Guildford Dudley.

Edward VI, on his deathbed, declared Jane to be the rightful Queen of England, much to the annoyance of Mary, a rightful descendant and Catholic.

The Protestant v Catholic 'see-saw' in England and a move to reinstate Mary as rightful heir, saw Jane imprisoned and the Crown taken from her.

Pressure from Catholics persuaded Mary to change her mind, and instead of keeping Jane alive, had her executed by beheading on the 12th of February 1554.

Here is her tale in verse –

Lady Jane Grey is my name, Lady Jane

A Queen for nine short days is my claim

I'm not wanted any more, the Executioner will call

and I'll lose my head for sure, I'm lady Jane

My name is Lady Jane, Lady Jane

Bradgate was my happy home, where I did play

In the park with dogs I'd roam, I'd be happier left alone

But I'm wanted on the throne, I'm Lady Jane

Nearly Queen one time before, I'm Lady Jane

Then came Dudley to my door, Lady Jane

He needs me on the throne, puppet marriage plans he's honed

Guilford Dudley is my troth, I'm Lady Jane

July 1553 I took the throne, now Queen Jane

But it only lasts nine days, what a pain

Mary's took it off of me but she's shown me clemency

So It's Lady Jane again, Lady Jane

But they still see me as a threat, Lady Jane

And now they want me dead, Lady Jane

So in 1554, I will lose my pretty head

On a block inside the Tower, Lady Jane

The Blue Boar Inn

Blue Boar Lane, until recently, was only visible through an old street sign on a wall adjoining a factory entrance on Highcross Street, and would have joined what is now Vaughan Way. The sign, gateway and reminder are now gone, having made way for new buildings.

The Inn had a chequered history, infamous for its 'colour changes' during the Wars of the Roses, and its most famous guest, King Richard III on the eve of the Battle of Bosworth in 1485.

The White Boar, The Blue Boar – Boar but never boring, as can be seen in this short tale-

There once was a tavern, they called the Blue Boar

Name retention was always a fight

It sat on a lane near the Holiday Inn

T'was a good resting place for the night

King Richard the Third came to Leicester to stay

And the Blue Boar turned quick to 'rose white'

To Bosworth he left for, the very next day

Heading off for his very last fight

When passing Bow Bridge, which he struck with his spur

Legend says Old Black Annis was there

She foretold his fate - and so it is said

On the same spot his dead head would strike - on return

In battle he died near to Bosworth they say

And his body was hauled back the opposite way

Towards the Blue Boar Inn he made his last ride

And at Bow Bridge his head struck that very same site!

The Blue Boar was trouble for some who there stayed

As found over the years, several folk

Like Alice Grimbold, a maid at the Inn

Who would end up in fire and in smoke

Alice was greedy and mackled a plan,

With a man called Harrison, slimy and broke

To murder a patron – poor old Agnes Clarke

To steal all her gold and elope

The plan went astry - and both thieves got caught

And death was to be their grim date

Alice burned at the stake in 1604

The last woman to suffer that fate!

And now the Blue Boar Inn

The lane where it stood - or its grounds

Where Richard and Agnes last rested their heads

On a map can no longer be found

A plaque marks the spot where Richard's head struck

His body newly found quite close by

Alice and Agnes – just remembered in Books

Blue Boar Lane - buried nearby the Shires

The last man in the Gibbet

On the 30th of May 1832, James Cook, a twenty one year old book-binder, with premises on Wellington Street, Leicester, murdered James Paas, of London.

A fire was discovered at Cook's premises, and on close inspection a large piece of meat was found burning in the hearth, which Cook alleged was meat for his dog.

Enquiries revealed other evidence, and the meat was the remains of Mr Paas.

Cook, in the meantime had fled Leicester, and was on his way via a rowing boat, to board the 'Carle of Carlton', at Liverpool, bound for America.

Pursued, he jumped overboard, but was detained after swimming to the shore.

Convicted of Murder, Cook was executed on August 10th 1832, and after execution, his body was placed in a gibbet cage at the junction of Saffron Lane and Aylestone Road.

He was the last man in the gibbet in Leicestershire.

Here is his tale.

'James Cook' – he heard the Judge call out

'You'll go from here to whence you came

You'll only stop at Leicester Gaol

To feel the hangman's pain'

The gallery heard those chilling words

'Then to the Gibbet post

Where your remains will stay

As a lesson to us all'

A heinous crime he did commit

He murdered poor John Paas

He chopped him into little bits

And cooked him on the hearth

Cook's neck was stretched that fateful day

His head then shaved and tarred

To preserve it from the weather

Inside the gibbet bars

On Saffron Lane the Gibbet stood

Near to the Aylestone Road

His body chained with hooded face

Was hauled into its place

The Gibbet – a deterrent?

I really think not much

A thousand people came and watched

As Cook became crows' lunch

Within a week - this ghastly scene

The cage got taken down

And ne'er again a Gibbet used

Near to old Leicester town

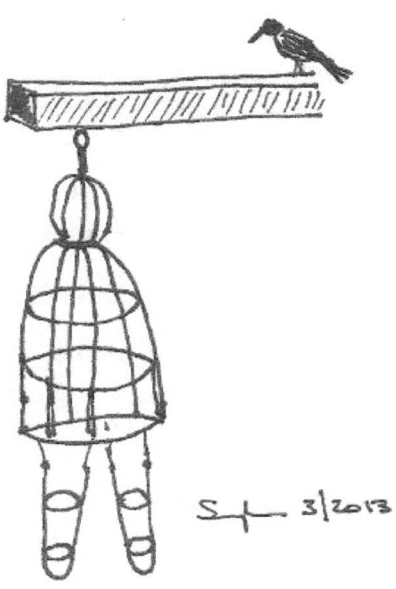

S+ 3/2013

George Davenport – Highwayman

A much maligned legend, George Davenport, to many was *'The other Robin Hood'*.

A family man, with a devoted wife; for 18 years he plied his trade on Leicestershire roads and highways, as a Highwayman.

He more often than not, used his gains, to look after those needier than he himself.

He was loved in Wigston, where his reputation for boisterous nights dancing on the roof of the Old Crown Inn, on Moat Street, originates.

Finally caught near to Loughborough, he was caught, tried and executed, barbarically it is alleged, as his neck was not broken, but stretched.

His remains are buried in All Saints Church in Wigston Magna, unknown to all but a few.

Here is his tale -

At All Saints in Wigston says the legend, for sure

Is a small patch of ground – hard to see any more

There lieth the bones of one Davenport, George

Despised by the rich but admired by the poor

What made a young boy take up mask and gun?

Was it something the parents or religion had done?

But the mask and the gun became tools of his trade

'Til the end in this cold ground his body was laid

There wasn't a road for miles round he ignored

With pistol and stallion, fine wealth he had scored

He took it to Wigston and shared with the poor

Like Robin Hood 'fore him, a rogue they adored

He raced from his hold ups on his stallion, fleet hoofed

To the Old Crown in Wigston where he danced on the roof

To the joy of the poor and the fear of the rich

What would lead to the end of this Highwayman's itch?

1797 saw that fatal mistake, when a journeyman butcher

Cudgeled George on the head

He bound him up tightly, like he tied joints of beef

And then handed him over - now soon he'd be dead

When the end came as normal for Highwaymen bold

T'was as expected - on the old Gallows' pole

Where he swung as a lesson to others - the thought

Even Highwaymen liked are eventually caught

So now he lies cold in an overgrown grave

Just old bones and a legend of one once so brave

In a part of Old Wigston, known to only a few

The end of the legend? That isn't quite true

If you're passing through Wistow and you feel a chill shiver

Keep an eye on the roadside, so others have said

You may hear someone call out 'Heed - Stand and deliver!'

It'll be Ghostly George - cos' he don't know he's dead

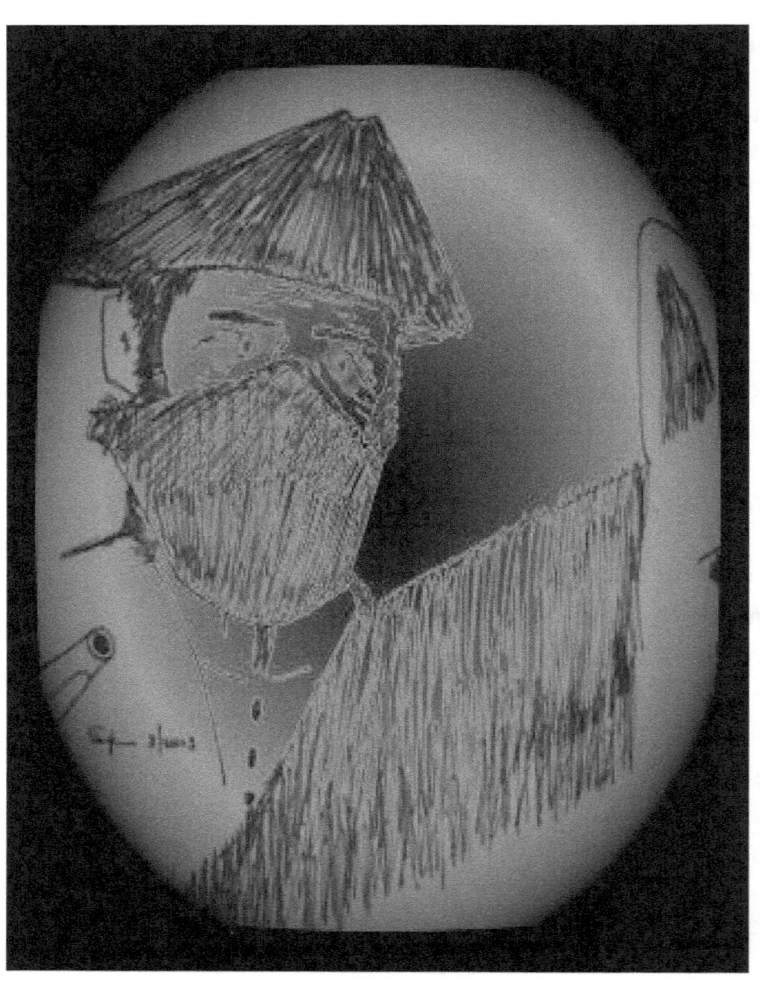

Joseph Carey (aka 'John') Merrick – The Elephant man

Born on the 5th of August 1860 (some records suggest 1862), in Lee Street, Leicester.

Within the first two years of birth Joseph developed Tumours, which were to give him the look and name of 'Elephant Man'.

For a long time it was unclear what his actual condition was, and today, after DNA testing, it is still unclear.

The general consensus is that he suffered from neurofibromatosis type I and Proteus syndrome.

A picture paints a thousand words.

What Joseph Merrick had to suffer, in verse

-

Poor old John Merrick he suffered a curse

Born with a condition they couldn't reverse

With pustules and tumours, detested and feared

Poor old John Merrick couldn't find things much worse

'Look away, Look away', the mothers were heard

As women and children all ran away scared

'That's what we call the Elephant man

Run away or he'll get you, as fast as you can'

Victorian Leicester was no place to hide

Wharf Street a notorious home to abide

With Vagrants, and Prostitutes, Drunkards and thieves

John took off to London his grotesque disease

Much to the Capital's perverse delight

John Merrick turned out a most curious sight

Amongst bearded ladies and on freak-show boards

He soon found his curse brought both fame and reward

'Look here, Look here', the audience cried

As Men, women and children, the freak-show they tried

'Now that's what they call Leicester's 'Elephant man'

Go tell of, to others, as fast as you can'

And so the name stuck - John found fortune and fame

A blue plaque on a wall only bears his true name

'A true model of bravery and dignity' how he's described

But 'the Elephant man' - no doubt, is how he'll remain

www.ingramcontent.com/pod-product-compliance
Lightning Source LLC
Chambersburg PA
CBHW070507290526
45790CB00003B/1133